THE PERFECTION
STORM

SEVEN STEPS TO GO
THROUGH A STORM

MARCIA CHRISTIAN BELL

WESTBOW
P R E S S®
A DIVISION OF THOMAS NELSON
& ZONDERVAN

Scripture taken from the New King James Version®. Copyright © 1982
by Thomas Nelson. Used by permission. All rights reserved.

This book is a work of non-fiction. Unless otherwise noted, the author and the publisher
make no explicit guarantees as to the accuracy of the information contained in this book
and in some cases, names of people and places have been altered to protect their privacy.

WestBow Press books may be ordered through booksellers or by contacting:

WestBow Press
A Division of Thomas Nelson & Zondervan
1663 Liberty Drive
Bloomington, IN 47403
www.westbowpress.com
1 (866) 928-1240

Because of the dynamic nature of the Internet, any web addresses or links contained in
this book may have changed since publication and may no longer be valid. The views
expressed in this work are solely those of the author and do not necessarily reflect the
views of the publisher, and the publisher hereby disclaims any responsibility for them.

Any people depicted in stock imagery provided by Thinkstock are models,
and such images are being used for illustrative purposes only.
Certain stock imagery © Thinkstock.

ISBN: 978-1-5127-9256-0 (sc)
ISBN: 978-1-5127-9257-7 (e)

Print information available on the last page.

WestBow Press rev. date: 07/03/2017

To all of my family members who are now in glory, and who left a legacy of strength and honor, teaching me that life is full of storms that don't come to harm you but to give you strength.

To my husband Barney and children, Marquis, Morshawn, Trelane, Rici, and Phil, for being my main source of strength. To my son, Aaron, who is now in glory, for being my main point of inspiration to re-write my book on the Perfection Storm.

To my sisters, brothers, nieces, nephews and most of all, my grandchildren, including the rest of my family and those who loved and believed in me and all that I do.

Contents

Foreword

Everyone experiences storms, lots of them. People, organization, and cities have experienced them. And Marcia Christian Bell has experienced them. I believe that storms are inevitable and intended to cleanse us and call us closer to the God of the storm. They are not intended to kill us. In *The Perfection Storm*, Bell, our ship's captain, encourages us and guides us through some of the most challenging moments of our lives. Using Paul's shipwreck in Acts, she roots her own story in the biblical narrative that helps us all locate ourselves in the great story of God.

If you will allow God to use this book amidst this difficult moment in your life, you will realize that God intends for this storm to make you a better grandfather, mother, son, co-worker, and neighbor. May this storm have a perfecting effect upon your life.

Phil Skei, Neighborhood Revitalization Manager,
Co-Pastor, On Ramps Covenant Church, Fresno California

Preface

I was inspired to rewrite this book on the Perfection Storm, because on September 30th of 2015, I lost my youngest son, Aaron Bell, to ARLD (Alcohol Related Liver Disease), which was triggered by situational depression caused by a broken court order and he became dependant upon alcohol to get him through the day to numb his pain. Although, my original thought was to help others in their time of need as they go through some of these wicked storms in life, I had no clue that this storm, of losing my son, was in my forecast. Although God is perfect in all of His ways, sometimes it takes a crisis to get your attention. He may not have sent the storm, but God will use it for His glory.

I entered a time where I didn't want to hear Scriptures like Romans 8:28, "For we know that all things work together for the good, to them that loved the Lord and are called according to His purpose" or 1 Peter 5:7, 10b. "Cast your cares on Him, for He cares for you ... After you have suffered just a little while, He will perfect or mature you, establish, strengthen and settle you." I didn't want to be strengthened in this way of losing my son to death. And lastly, this was a time that I didn't want to hear James 1:2-4 when it tells you to "count it all joy when you go through various trials, knowing that it's the testing of your faith that produces patience and your patience will have its perfect work. That you may be perfect or mature and complete in whatever it is and you won't lack anything."

I'm just being transparent. I didn't want my son's death to work for my good. I sure didn't want to cast my cares on the Lord for Him to mature me or establish me and settle me. And lastly, I didn't want patience to be produced in my life and have its perfect work in me. I didn't want to be made perfect and complete in this way. I knew what all the scriptures said. I just wanted my son back! At that moment, as the Word commands me to count it all joy, I couldn't count this all joy, because this wasn't joyful at all. But in the deep recesses of my mind, I knew that this didn't take God by surprise and He would bring me through this.

I will never forget that day when I was watching television, some years ago, on one of the Christian stations, and heard the preacher say something about Paul going through a storm. I remember how on that day, it prompted me to read Acts 27 when I discovered seven things that Paul went through while he was on a ship headed toward Rome and went head-on into a storm. I didn't realize that I was going to need this book in my life. I thought I was already in a storm then but that was nothing compared to what I had to go through on September 30 2015. I was going to need to read my own book on how to get through this storm of when my son died and that I would never in a million years begin to phathom that this would be in my forecast. Of course, this only happened to other people. Not me!

For the last year, as I thought about the content of what kind of new information I would put into this book, I began to realize that I was in a season of "stand still and know that I am God" (Ps.46:10 NKJV). My child had died and I couldn't see what God was doing. Although I had trusted God, I also felt betrayed by God all at the same time. God knew how I had been faithful to Him and how I took great care of everybody else and now my child had to die. I was faithful to pray for others, I brought my children up in the fear and admonition of the Lord, I taught others the Word of God, mentored others, fed people continuously and so much more. And now Lord, You're taking my child from me? I was paralyzed. I couldn't turn to the left or to the right, I couldn't move forward, yet I was not going to move backward. My direction wasn't clear because I had shed so many tears, angry at God, confused, happy and sad all at the same time and the heavy rains were everywhere and I couldn't see. So the rewriting of this book began to take on a different shape for me.

Introduction

I was in a situation where I felt like my world was going to come crumbling down right before my eyes? Everywhere I turned, I couldn't cry out like I wanted to. Although family and friends were there for me, I didn't want to be in this time of grieving for my son in front of them. After all, I had to be strong. At least that's what people say. I knew that as I had to get through the next few days preparing for my son's home-going celebration, I felt like I couldn't breathe or I was in a dream. Everything was so surreal. I knew that (James 1:2 NKJV) told me to "count it all joy," this was not a joyful time. Rather, it was painful, but God promised that I would receive the peaceful fruit of righteousness because I was being trained for something bigger (Heb. 12:11NKJV).

I now have a new normal and I had to accept the fact that there are no do-overs in this new normal. I can't say, I wished I had of done or said this or that. My life will be forever changed, so I had to continue to reflect on (Acts 27 NKJV), to remind myself on what Paul had to endure while he was in his storm. I began to meditate on the events that led up to my storm and I even asked the question of why am I in this situation? So let's look at Paul again and see what he did in his storm and then apply these principles in our lives and watch God work. Remember this one thing as you read *The Perfection Storm*. "Things are not where they are supposed to be after a storm passes. Storms come to mess things up" (Elmer Towns). But God loves to clean up messes and give us a new message.

What Is a Storm?

Before we dive into this reading, I want to go into detail about what a storm is and what the travelers had to deal with in Acts 27. The *World Book Encyclopedia* describes storms as atmospheric cyclones that are low-pressure areas circled by winds that spiral inward, and if there is little or no moisture in the air, a cyclone may travel a great distance without bringing precipitation. But if a cyclone meets a mass of warm, humid air, the swirling winds draw it in.

The moist air rises in the low-pressure center and then cools and condenses or sublimes. Drops, flakes, and ice crystals form. When they grow heavy enough, they fall to the ground. We call it hail. I want you to picture this in your Holy Ghost imagination because, in the passage of Scripture we will examine, this was a tremendous storm that the travelers had to endure for two weeks.

We find this same kind of storm in (Mark 4:37–41 NKJV) when Jesus and the disciples were crossing over to the other side and a storm arose. The waves were beating into the ship, filling it up, while Jesus was fast asleep at the stern. The disciples forgot that the Prince of Peace was on the boat with them. After they woke up Jesus for fear that they would drown, He spoke these words, "Peace, be still." A great calm took over the situation. This same calm will come into your storm when Jesus speaks a word.

Why Seven Steps?

I discovered that Paul and his traveling companions did seven things while they were in this storm, and we will adventure together to learn to incorporate these successful seven things they did in order to go through our own storms into our lives. You may ask, "Why does there have to be steps at all?" (Psalm 37:23 NKJV) contains the answer to your question. "The steps of a good man are ordered by the Lord." Also, the biblical significance of the number seven is perfection or completeness. You want to be perfect and complete, lacking nothing, don't you? The following are some Scriptures on the number seven that are divinely mentioned in the Bible:

- God ended his work and rested on the seventh day (Gen. 2:2 NKJV).
- Naaman dipped in the Jordan River seven times and was healed of his leprosy (2 Kings 5:10, 14 NKJV).
- The Shunamite woman's son sneezed seven times and came back to life (2 Kings 4:35 NKJV).
- The woman at the well had five husbands, she was living with the sixth man, and then Jesus, the seventh man, came along and made her life complete (John 4:16–18 NKJV). She came out of that lifestyle and became an evangelist in her own hometown.

These are just a few passages, but the list goes on and on. As you complete reading *The Perfection Storm* in seven hours, seven days or seven weeks, remember that (James 1:4 NKJV) commands us to let "patience do its perfect work." Then you can become perfect, complete, and lacking in nothing after you've counted it all joy when you fall into various trials because it will produce your patience.

Let's begin the journey to discover our seven steps in our Perfection Storm. I pray this book will bless you as richly as it has blessed me in the gathering of this valuable information, and I hope you will get information along with revelation and a sense of destiny and direction.

As you read, keep in mind that a storm is a strong wind with rain, snow, hail, or thunder and lightning. Some of these things you thought were surely not in your forecast but here they are. I know you don't want to be in this storm, and you want to get out of it. Remember, (Ps. 107:29 NKJV) reminds us that "God calms the storm, so that its waves are still." Also, (Phil. 4:7 NKJV) consoles us saying, "The peace of God, which surpasses all understanding, will guard your hearts and minds through Christ Jesus."

STEP ONE

When the south wind blew softly, supposing that they had obtained their desire, putting out to sea, they sailed close by Crete. But not long after, a tempestuous head wind arose, called Euroclydon. So when the ship was caught, and could not head into the wind, we let her drive.
(Acts 27:15 NKJV)

Let Her Drive

In this life, I have been in unpleasant or destructive situations or circumstances that consisted of rain, snow, sleet, and hail. I've even been in strong winds that were forcing me to go with the flow? Most of the time, I had no control over the situation. I only knew that I didn't want to be nowhere near it and I wanted to be somewhere safe and in a warm place. I remember years ago when a friend of mine was driving on a rainy day and her car hit some black ice. She began skidding out of control. In order for her to come out of that situation, she had to turn the steering wheel in the direction that the car was going and she hit the embankment and it stopped her car. This is what the travelers had to do while in the ship. They couldn't turn the ship into the wind so they gave up and had to go into the direction that the ship was going and be driven along. Sometimes, there is nothing you can do about the direction your life is going. I surely did not want life to go in the direction it was going for me. My son's death was not supposed to happen. This happened to other families, but we had to accept what the Lord was doing and continue to give Him the glory because He is still the supreme ruler. He's going to do what He wants to do, when He wants to do it and how He wants to do it. He chose to take my son, Aaron, home to be with Him on that day, at that time and in that way.

Set Sail

(Acts 27:13 NKJV) tells us that there was calmness over the sea and a breeze that blew softly from the south in the morning, so they set sail quickly, hugging the shoreline for protection. It's just like when you're doing something you know you have no business doing, but you've convinced yourself that it's okay for now. Then suddenly things began to go out of your control and it prevented you from moving forward and flourishing the way God had intended for you. Scripture says, suddenly, a violent northeasterly storm called Euroclydon hit the ship, preventing the crew from sailing into the wind. Keep this in your mind. The travelers were sailing at the wrong time of the year and had no business out there in the waters. When you're out of the will of God, it will not be a good outcome.

The storm drove the ship south of a small island named Clauda, which broke the force of the wind long enough for the crew to take some measures to secure the ship. When in my storm, I had to renew my thoughts, my heart, and my mind. I had to secure my ship. As (1 Cor. 5:18 NKJV) says, I was no longer the old Marcia, I was the new Marcia with a new normal and a new found dependence upon the Lord for His strength in my circumstance. In addition to that, our church was in a corporate fast for two weeks when my storm happened. My prayer life and my praise changed, along with many other things in my life. I even began to think of Heaven more often now because I knew it was my son Aaron's new home.

(2 Chronicles 20 NKJV) gives the narrative of when King Jehoshaphat got word that the enemy was coming up against his people to destroy them (inhabitants of Judah). "Now when they began to sing and praise, the Lord set ambushes against the people of Ammon, Moab, and Mount Seir." I began to praise the Lord in spite of my circumstance. The enemy thought he was going to destroy me but my

praise became my weapon against him. I did this with tears running down my face trying to smile at my son's pictures. That's when I began to attend GriefShare ministries and I learned how to grieve well and learn how to smile again. God set ambushes against the enemy on my behalf with His words of comfort.

(Acts 27:15 NKJV) says that, when the ship was caught and unable to bear up against the wind, they gave up fighting against the direction of the wind and began to drift. They tried to secure the skiff on deck with a tremendous amount of difficulty. We need to learn how to stop trying to hold on to stuff when you're already going through a storm. Your load is already too heavy and you're going to try to hold onto it during your storm. As we go into 2017, we need to let go of some things that will cause us to hold onto some unhealthy things and toxic relationships as well.

The man at the pool of Bethesda hung around the wrong people for thirty-eight years (John 5:1–8 NKJV). He hung around the blind, the lame, and the paralyzed and he had an infirmity to top it all off. As soon as Jesus came into his life and he heard and obeyed him, his healing came, and he took his bed and got up off the ground at that very moment and began to walk. Essentially, you must let go of some stuff so there won't be any hinderances as you walk into your destiny. You don't want anything, including the wrong people holding you back.

(Acts 27:15 NKJV) continues to tell us that, when they hoisted the skiff on deck, they used ropes to try to undergird and brace the ship. They feared they would be driven into the quicksands of Syrtis, so they lowered the sails and ropes and let the ship drive.

Spiritual Drifting

To be driven, here in this section, means to drift with the force of the wind. Your first step is to flow or drift with the direction of your storm or flow with the anointing that's in your life right now. (Romans 8:28 NKJV) tells us, "For we know that all things work together for good to them that love the Lord and are called according to His purpose." This is not talking about a drifting away, but moving into the direction of your breakthrough. You may think it's a negative thing to drift or to be carried along with the currents of life, but don't fret when the wind and waves seem to take you in a direction that you didn't want to go and you think there is no purpose in it for you. Take the time to look back at your life then begin to see how you've overcome some storms and how you've learned from them. Can you see that you're not in the same place you used to be?

In case you need more of an explanation on spiritual drifting, I will show you some profiles of people who had to spiritually drift into their divine destiny.

- Moses hadn't planned on killing the Egyptian, fleeing into the desert, and then staying there for forty years. Little did he know that he was training in the desert to be the deliverer of the children of Israel and lead them out of bondage in Egypt. With some resistance and a few excuses, he spiritually drifted into his position (Exodus 2:11–12, 14 NKJV).
- Mary, the mother of Jesus, hadn't planned on being pregnant while betrothed to Joseph. She was to be the mother of the Messiah, the Savior of the world. Can you imagine the drama she went through being an unwed mother? Talk about spiritually drifting as she submissively took on her role. She was very submissive to the work of the Holy Spirit that had come upon her and overshadowed her, which also included submitting her body to the will of the Father. Remember, she was just a peasant girl and a commoner who went to the well daily to walk into her destiny of being "blessed and highly favored" (Luke 1:26–38 NKJV).
- Gideon, who had low self-esteem, as evidenced by him saying, "My clan is the weakest in Manasseh, and I am the least in my father's house," was called by his name of destiny. God exalted him and called him "you mighty man of Valor." God called him into courage, boldness, bravery, worthiness, and strength in battle, and he was valuable. With God's strategic instructions,

Gideon defeated the countless number of Midianites with only three hundred of his men (Judges 6–7 NKJV).

- Jonah was told to go to Ninevah and preach repentance that leads to salvation to his enemies, the Assyrians. Jonah refused and went the opposite direction, thinking he could get away from the Lord's presence. Well, he spent three days and three nights, in the belly of a large fish. God sent him into his own private storm. Although Jonah realized he brought on his own storm, which we do the same, he spiritually drifted into his God-appointed calling. Jonah's experience in the belly of the fish is parallel to Jesus' death, burial, and resurrection. (Jonah 1:17, Matt. 12:38–41 NKJV)

These are just a few profiles of individuals who God Himself called. They spiritually drifted into their divine destiny to carry out God's purpose and their God-appointed role.

Purpose in Pain

You might be asking right now, "Did they have to go through all that?" You may not see it now, and you sure don't want to be in it, but there is purpose in your pain, too. When my son passed away, I knew what the scriptures said about my pain. I knew that God was going to give me beauty for my ashes and joy for my spirit of heaviness and He has. Please know that (Jeremiah 29:11 NKJV) will remind you that God sees you in your situation. His plans were not to harm me. He saw me in my situation and said to me, "Daughter" "For I know the thoughts that I think toward you, says the Lord, thoughts of peace and not of evil, to give you a future and a hope."

God was getting me ready for my next level of faith. I found out through 12 weeks of counseling that I didn't have to be strong. His strength would be made perfect in my weakness. I had to go through this storm whether I wanted to or not. There was no turning back or no do overs. He predestined me before the foundation of the world to do the supernatural. My pain was not going to drop to the ground.

I had to live with joy and pain all at the same time, and that He was going to reward me with promise and purpose and I intend to use it for God's glory!

God's thoughts are not your thoughts, nor are your ways, His ways, says the Lord." (Isa. 55:8 NKJV). There is no way that I would have planned this for myself. God, in His infinite ways, has already gone to eternity and back for me and knew there would be a good outcome. He knows the end from the beginning. He hasn't closed his eyes concerning you. His name is El Roi, which means He sees everything. Remember, nothing takes God by surprise, and He has already seen it. He's omniscient, so He already knows what's going to happen He's omnipresent, which means He's everywhere at the same time. And last of all, He has you covered, and He has not forgotten you, although you may feel differently.

God's Permissive Will

Keep in mind that God, in His permissive will, is going to allow a storm to come up against you. God allowed this storm to enter into my life. A storm will come whether you want it to or not. You might as well make a decision to learn from it. I now look at the book of Job with a different set of eyes. And I've asked the question, "Why me? And why did I have to go through all of this? Why did my son have to die?"

I have to keep repeating to myself again and again (James 1:2–4 NKJV). It tells me to "count it all joy when you fall into various trials, knowing that the testing of your faith produces patience. But let patience have its perfect work, that you may be perfect and complete, lacking nothing." In other words, the work of patience has to be completed so I wouldn't lack anything, and I had to accept the fact that this was my new normal and nothing was going to change other than my new found faith in God.

Another scripture that God had to instill in my spirit was, "When you pass through the waters, I will be with you; and through the rivers, they shall not overflow you. When you walk through the fire, you shall not be burned, nor shall the flame scorch you" (Isa. 43:2 NKJV). In other words, God was telling me that, whatever I'm going through, He's right there with me and you. We need to keep our focus on Him no matter what. Finally, remember (Ps. 34:19 NKJV). "The righteous suffer many afflictions, tests and trials, but our God delivers us out of all of them." Isn't that good to know?

You Will Be Delivered

Remember (Ps. 91:3 NKJV). "He will deliver you from the snare of the fowler." Also remember (1 Peter 5:10 NKJV). "But may the God of all grace, who called us to His eternal glory by Christ Jesus, after you have suffered a while will perfect, establish, strengthen, and settle you." The Amplified Bible interprets it to say, "And after you have suffered a little while, the God of all grace (who imparts all blessing and favor). Who has called you to His eternal glory in Christ Jesus, will Himself complete and make you what you ought to be, establish and ground you securely, and strengthen and settle you."

And you thought God forgot about you. God has not forgotten you and will not pass you by (Mark 6:48 NKJV). "His thoughts are precious towards us and the sum of them are great" (Ps. 139:17 NKJV). He even knows the number of hairs on our heads. Don't worry. He's got your back! Remember the words of David, "The Lord is my shepherd, I shall not want. He makes me to lie down in green pastures; He leads me beside the still waters. He restores my soul; he leads me in the paths of righteousness for His name's sake. Yea, though I walk through the valley of the shadow of death, I will fear no evil; for You are with me; Your rod and Your staff, they comfort me. You prepare a table before me in the presence of my enemies; You anoint my head with oil; My cup runs over. Surely goodness and mercy shall follow me all the days of my life; and I will dwell in the house of the Lord forever." (Ps. 23 NKJV).

List some things that you need to spiritually drift into:

1. _____

2. _____

3. _____

4. _____

Remember, you are spiritually drifting when you're going through a storm. You're going with the direction and flow of the Holy Spirit and the anointing of God. You have a divine purpose, a divine plan for your life, and a divine destiny. Don't be like Jonah and spend more time in the belly of a fish than you ought to getting to your assignment. He brought on his own storm with his disobedience and the way to punish disobedience is with obedience (2 Cor. 10:6 NKJV). Sounds too simple, don't you think?

Father in heaven, help me to know when I am spiritually drifting into my divine destiny and purpose while in my storm. Help me to stay on course with the flow of the anointing. Teach me, O God, to recognize You and know You are present with me. I pray this prayer in the mighty name of your Son, Jesus. Amen!

STEP TWO

And because we were exceedingly tempest-tossed, the next
day they lightened the ship. On the third day we threw
the ship's tackle overboard with our own hands.
(Acts 27:18–19 NKJV)

Throw Some Stuff Overboard

Acts says that, on the second day, Paul and the other travelers began to lighten the ship and throw some stuff overboard, the ship's tackle. They realized that in order to survive the storm they had to get rid of some things that were going to make their struggle more cumbersome. The prisoners discovered very quickly that anything that was ineffective needed to be thrown out of their way with their own hands.

There are some storms that you're going to have to handle with your own hands. You can either be defeated in the storm or help your own self by throwing some things out of your life so that it won't be so difficult. A similar story in the book of (Jonah 1:5 NKJV), the mariners began to throw the ship's cargo overboard to lighten the ship because of their storm. Finally, they realized that Jonah was the cargo they needed to throw overboard. Let me pause here and ask you, "What's the name of your Jonah that you need to throw overboard while you're in this tempest tossed storm?" Make it easy on yourself. Storms don't come to stay, they come to pass

The storm you're in is sufficient of itself. Why are you trying to carry a heavy load of excess weight right along with it? (Hebrews 12:1

NKJV) says to "lay aside every weight, and the sin which so easily ensnarcs us, and let us run with endurance the race that is set before us." The Amplified Bible says "Let us strip off and throw aside every encumbrance and that sin which so readily clings to and entangles us, and let us run with patient endurance and steady and active persistence the appointed course of the race that is set before us."

How can you run a race with weights on and expect to win? It's impossible. Even a sprinter in a race makes sure he attains the proper weight and is conditioned to win the race. Paul says, "Brethren, I do not count myself to have apprehended; but one thing I do, forgetting those things which are behind and reaching forward to those things which are ahead, I press towards the goal for the prize of the high calling of God in Christ Jesus" (Phil. 3:13 NKJV). You have to move forward with nothing in your way or holding you back. You may stumble, but even if you do, stumble forward in the direction of your breakthrough.

Identifying Weights

Let me help you identify some weighty things that need to be layed aside and thrown overboard according to (Gal. 5:19–21 NKJV). It warns us about the doings of the flesh that are very clear. They speak of the four I's: immorality, impurity, indecency and idolatry. In other words, worshipping something that is wicked and contaminated that will create strongholds in your life that need to be stripped away. The other elements that need to be layed aside are: sorcery, enmity, strife, jealousy, anger and selfishness. These elements create bitter roots.

The last group that needs to be thrown overboard are: divisions, party spirit, envy, drunkenness, carousing. They bring about darkness. Although this scripture isn't inclusive, none of these things will help you in your tempest tossed storm. In fact, these weighty things or cargo will keep you in the storm longer than you want to stay, take you to places you don't want to go, and cost you more than you want to pay.

You need to begin to list some things that are weighing on you and making your load heavier than you want it to be. Some of these things have names and places. Jesus said in (Matt. 11:28–30 NKJV), "Come to Me, all you who labor and are heavy laden, and I will give you rest. Take my yoke upon you and learn from Me, for I am gentle and lowly in heart, and you will find rest for your souls. For My yoke is easy and My burden is light." Without any question, some of you reading this right now know you need some rest from that storm, which is a person, place, or thing, right now, yesterday, and immediately. Your very life depends on it.

Casting Off

Pick up that unnecessary stuff and throw it as hard and far as you can. You've spent too much precious time holding onto it. (Rom. 13:12–14 NKJV) says, "The night is far spent, the day is at hand, therefore let us cast off the works of darkness, and let us put on the armor of light. Let us walk properly, as in the day, not in revelry and drunkenness, not in lewdness and lust, not in strife and envy. But put on the Lord Jesus Christ, and make no provision for the flesh, to fulfill its lusts." (1 Peter 5:7 NKJV) demands that we "cast your cares upon the Lord, for He cares for you."

Pastor Paula White says a care is like a boulder that you carry on you back. Can you imagine a boulder on your back everywhere you go? And Jesus said for us to cast it. It sounds like we need to make some serious adjustments. It begins with a renewed mind. I've often heard it said, "You can't continue to do the same thing over and over and expect to get a different result. It's called insanity."

Renewing Your Mind

Several things I personally needed to throw overboard in the last several years were doubt, fear, unbelief, toxic relationships, and, as Joyce Meyers says, "stinking thinking." You have to let some people go. You have to start flying with eagles and not hang out with the turkeys and the chickens. They get eaten!

Some people or things will get in the way of your breakthrough. Ask the man at the Pool of Bethseda in (John 5:1–8 NKJV). He was at the pool for thirty-eight years, hanging around people who were lame, blind, and paralyzed. He waited every year at the same time for the water to be stirred. This was the time of year when one person would be healed. Then one day, Jesus came around and asked him, "Do you want to be healed?" The man gave Jesus an excuse, like we do at times, and said, "No man put me in the water when it is stirred." Jesus just told him, "Get up, take up your bed, and walk." That's all it took for this man to get his breakthrough. He had to let some people and some things go and stop listening to negative talk. He had to change who he was hanging around with and make up in his mind that he was going to change his own outcome.

I also had to throw overboard some hurtful talking. You might be thinking right now, "You did some hurtful talking?" Yes, I did, and so did you. I had to speak to my storm of losing my son and tell it to be still. I had to remind myself that peace was in the boat, and his name is Jesus. Instead of saying things like "I'll never get over this storm because people don't get over losing their child." I had to learn that this was my new normal and remember that it would only be God's Word that was going to heal my broken heart. Neither could I let any corrupt words come out of my mouth. Only words that were good for necessary edification that would impart grace or favor to those that would hear me speak (Eph. 4:29 NKJV). Even to myself.

We need to take the time to encourage ourselves like King David did. Scripture tells us, "Now David was greatly distressed, for the people spoke of stoning him, because the soul of all the people was grieved, every man for his sons and his daughters. But David strengthened himself in the Lord his God." (1 Sam. 30:6 NKJV).

(Prov. 18:21 NKJV) says, "There is life and death in the power of the tongue and if you love it, you will eat of its fruit." You have to speak life into your situation. God says, "I set before you this day, life and death, good and evil" (Deut. 30:15 NKJV). It's too simple. Choose life. You know that old school saying, "Loose lips sink ships." I didn't want to sink my own ship with my own mouth by speaking words that were going to harm me. I also didn't want to be that foolish woman in (Prov. 14:1 NKJV) that says, "The wise woman builds her house, but the foolish pulls it down with her hands." In other words, build yourself up by prophesying to yourself with the word of God, and don't pull yourself down by focusing on the things of this world.

You can't be conformed to this world and its way of thinking, because the things of this world are temporal. Our minds need to be renewed (Rom. 12:2 NKJV). Whatever we think in our hearts, that's what we are. Scripture tells us in (Matt. 12:34 NKJV), "For out of the abundance of the heart, the mouth speaks". And yes, we are what we eat." What are you eating? I pray it's the Word.

If you think you're not going to make it, you're not. If you think you are going to make it, you are. (Rom. 4:17b NKJV) sums it all up by saying, "Call those things that be not as though they were." So in other words, call forth what you want to happen in your life, and it will obey you according to God's Word. I know that my life has changed forever, but I am determined to make it through moment by moment victoriously whether my eyes are filled with tears or otherwise.

The Ship's Tackle

Now that I have provoked your thoughts, why don't you take a few moments to identify some things you need to throw overboard and put them on a list? What's in your ship's tackle? First, let's break this down into three categories: tackle as in fishing tackle, tackle as in football, and tackle as in trying to deal with, solve, or master something that is very difficult.

Tackle, as in fishing tackle, will consist of the rod, line, ropes, hooks, and any other apparatus or fishing gear. Remember, you're already in a storm, and it's difficult to hold on to some things. List some things you are holding on to that you need to release:

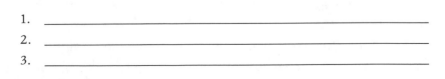

1. _____

2. _____

3. _____

Tackle, as in football, is an offensive or defensive player between the guard and the end on either side of the line. Who and what do you need to tackle? I suggest you sack the quarterback with your spiritual weapons. "The weapons of our warfare are not carnal but mighty in God for pulling down strongholds, casting down arguments and every high thing that exalts itself against the knowledge of God, bringing every thought into captivity to the obedience of Christ, and being ready to punish all disobedience when your obedience is fulfilled" (2 Cor. 10:4–6 NKJV).

The enemy gives all the plays against you. In the spirit realm, his name is Satan, and your offensive and defensive weapons are the "whole armor of God." I tell people that there are three things to do concerning the above-stated Scripture: capture it (that thought), pull it down, and punish it (disobedience). How do you punish disobedience?" The answer is, "With obedience." Start tackling. List some things you need to tackle:

1. _____

2. _____

3. _____

Tackle finally means as in trying to deal with, solve, or master something that is very difficult. What the travelers tried to use to secure the ship was in the tackle box. Throw it overboard. It's weighing you down. "Trust in the Lord with all your heart and lean not unto your own understanding. In all your ways acknowledge Him and He will direct your path" (Prov. 3:5–6 NKJV). What do you need to throw overboard?

The godly counsel I have for you is to do what James says. "Don't just hear the word, but be a doer of the word, because you're only deceiving yourself" (James 1:22–25 NKJV). You need to know that you hearing the Word, does not intimidate the devil. In fact, he knows the Word better than we do. Remember, he was with the Word in the wilderness, trying to tempt the Word with the Word (Matt. 4:1–11 NKJV). Satan gets intimidated when we start doing the Word. Hmm, this is something to ponder over.

Are you ready to go to the next step?

God in heaven, teach us, O God, to keep our eyes upon You. Teach us to cast our cares on You and lay aside things that distract us from Your purpose and will for our lives. Help us to renew our minds and begin to identify some weights that have tried to slow us down from reaching our destiny in You. O Lord, forgive us for trying to hang onto anything other than You. In Your Son's name, Amen!

STEP THREE

Now when neither sun nor stars appeared for many days, and no small
tempest beat on us, all hope that we would be saved was finally given up.
(Acts 27:20 NKJV)

Neither Sun Nor Stars

Have you ever been in a dark room and didn't know which direction to go for anything? You couldn't tell which way was north, south, east, or west. You couldn't remember where the door was. Perhaps you have knots on your forehead where you've bumped into the wall because you didn't wait for the light to be turned on. Start feeling your forehead now. Any knots? Hmm, I have a few.

I once went shopping at the mall. As I prepared to leave, I lost my sense of direction and couldn't remember which entrance I used or where I parked my car. As I stopped in my tracks, I looked around for something familiar, and I began to ask, "Which way should I go?" Then I remembered a Tremaine Hawkin's song that says, "What step should I take? What move should I make?" Then she goes on to sing, "I'm going to wait for an answer from You. I know you'll come through." It was like the lights had come on, and I began to move toward the correct exit and found my car.

All this sounds too familiar, doesn't it? Have you ever gotten lost while traveling without a map, compass, or GPS in your vehicle? Did you pull over and ask for directions? Or did you keep moving, hoping you were going in the right direction? Have you ever made a decision to do something you regretted and wished you had waited instead?

Sun and Stars for Direction

(Acts 27:20 NKJV) says, "That neither sun nor stars were visible for many days and the tempest was not small." The first step described the storm's condition. Because of the intensity of the storm, Paul and the others could not see the sun or stars. You can witness to the fact that, when it rains, you can't see the sun because of the dark clouds.

In times past, if they didn't use the sun and stars as a compass, they didn't know which direction to go. Even though they probably used maps and graphs, at this point, those instruments were not useful. The majority of the stars, including the sun, fell into one pattern. This was the main sequence, and when plotted on a graph according to luminosity and type of spectrum, they couldn't be seen. So they had no clue which direction to go.

We know that the sun rises in the east and sets in the west. Okay, that one was easy. Look at this. Scripture tells us that the Wise Men in (Matt. 2:1–12 NKJV) were from the East on their way to Jerusalem saying, "Where is He who has been born King of the Jews? For we have seen His star in the East and have come to worship Him." They were using the star as a compass to locate the Savior.

Sun and Stars for Timing

On the West Coast in the Central Valley of California, the sun begins to rise in the east during the summer at approximately five thirty in the morning and sets in the west at approximately seven in the evening. In the heat of the day, you can guess the time of the day is between noon and two in the afternoon. In other words, you can pretty much determine what time it is by the rising and setting of the sun.

(Matt. 2:7 NKJV) tells us that Herod secretly called the Wise Men into talk with him. After hearing them talk, he could determine the age of the newborn king and what time the star appeared. He knew that, by determining the time the star appeared, they were no longer looking for a baby. They were looking for a young child, approximately two years old.

(Matt. 2:16 NKJV) says that, after Herod realized the Wise Men had misled him, he ordered that all the male children two years old and younger be put to death. (Matt. 2:8 NKJV) tells us that Herod sent them to Bethlehem and told them, "Go and search for the young child (not a baby) and when you have found Him, bring Him back to me so I can worship Him also."

(Matt. 2:11 NKJV) says, "And when they had come into the house, they saw the young child with Mary His mother, and fell down and worshipped Him." Keep in mind that Joseph and Mary are no longer in a stable but are now in a house. After the Wise Men gave Jesus gifts and worshipped Him and were divinely instructed and warned in a dream not to return to Herod, their direction was changed.

So time and seasons have a lot to do with your situation, as quoted in (Ecc. 3:1–8 NKJV). It says, "To everything there is a season, a time for every pupose under heaven: A time to be born, and a time to die; A time to plant, and a time to pluck what is planted; A time to kill, and a time to heal: A time to break down, and a time to build up: A time to weep, and a time to laugh; A time to mourn, and a time to dance; A time to cast away stones, and a time to gather stones; A time to embrace and a time to refrain from embracing; A time to gain, and a time to lose; A time to keep, and a time to throw away; A time to tear, and a time to sew; A time to keep silence, and a time to speak; A time to love, and a time to hate; A time of war, and a time of peace." It was time for my life to have a new normal.

Set, Stand, See (Set Yourself)

I once knew a young man who had been called into the preaching ministry. He wanted to jump right in without any direction. I remember him being told that he couldn't just take off and then ask God, which way do I go? Even King David went back out into the fields after he was anointed as Israel's next king and waited for God to direct him. It's the same principle when you get to a crossroad with two arrows going in opposite directions. You begin to stare at them, not knowing what to do. You wait for directions. So why do we try to go in a particular direction and don't know where we're going? Now think about this. You're in a storm, and you can't see because of the intensity of the storm. So what do you do?

Here's your answer, "Set yourself, stand still and see the salvation of the Lord" (2 Chron. 20:17 NKJV). Set, stand, and see. I call them the "Three Musketeers of the Chronicles." Let's take an adventure and break them down.

The *World Book Dictionary* tells us to *set* means to "put in some place, position, condition for use, or to adjust according to a standard." You have to "set your mind on things above, not on things on the earth" (Col. 3:2 NKJV). You have to position yourself in the word of God. You may ask, "How do I do that?"

Scripture tells us, "And do not be conformed to this world, but be transformed by the renewing of your mind, that you may prove what is that good and acceptable and perfect will of God" (Rom. 12:2 NKJV). So the setting begins in your mind. As a believer, you need to experience a transformation (Gk. Metamorphoo), which is to literally change. It's a new way of thinking made possible through the power of the Holy Spirit. You have to adjust your thinking and begin to have the mind of Christ (Phil. 2:5 NKJV) by putting on Christ. As my older son Marquis says, "Put Jesus on like lotion."

How do you do that? Begin to saturate yourself with the word of God when you get up in the morning, drive to work, go to school, take your breaks, drive home, cook dinner, and prepare to go to bed. All these times, put on Christ. You might be thinking, "How am I going to have time to do all of that and saturate myself with the word of God?"

Get up extra early and read, meditate, and pray. Put on Christian television or worship music as you get ready for work or school. You are depositing the Word into your spirit so you can become a little King David when he said, "Thy Word have I hid in my heart so that I won't sin against thee" (Ps. 119:11 NKJV). You can't pull up out of your spirit what's not in there.

(Luke 6:45b NKJV) says, "Out of the abundance of the heart, the mouth speaks." What does your heart have an abundance of? If you don't make a deposit of God's Word, you can't make a withdrawal. Try to make a withdrawal at the bank one day, and see the results you get. In addition, you can take a devotional or a small Bible, now your Bible app on your phone and fit them into your purse or pocket to keep with you at all times. And repeat the same thing you did in the morning when you get home in the evening.

So in order to set your mind, affections, longings, and desires on things above, you have to adjust your thinking to the standards of God. And how are you going to know what His standards, laws, statutes, decrees, and commandments are until you get into His Word and put on Christ? There's no way for you to have a transformed mind until you take the proper steps.

Stand Still

Second, you will stand still. The meaning of *stand still* (Gk. Histemi) is to metaphorically "stand firm in the truth" (John 14:6 NKJV), "in grace" (Rom. 5:2 NKJV), "in the gospel" (1 Cor. 15:1 NKJV), "by thy faith" (Rom. 11:20 NKJV), and "to be established" (1 Pet. 5:10 NKJV). If you're not standing on the word of God, you are not standing on a firm foundation, and you will sink.

Did you ever watch cowboy movies as a little kid? Whenever someone fell in quicksand, they were okay as long as they stood still. Then someone would come along and throw out a tree branch. The one in distress would hold on to the branch, and the other person would save him by pulling him out. But if they kept moving about, they would begin to sink. So what are you saying? You have to stand still so God can come into your quicksand, give you a Holy Ghost branch, and save you and pull you out of your stuff.

Waiting is a hard thing to do. We want to be a mini Holy Spirit and fix it ourselves because we think we have all the answers. I'm clearing my throat right now because I have been guilty of this on many occasions. I found out that while you are waiting, in the meantime, is a mean time. It's hard to manage, troublesome, vicious, and cruel. It gets rough and tough, and you feel like giving up.

Even though people say they're praying for you, they're interceding for you, and they've got your back, they really don't identify with your sufferings because it's not them. They want to see you come through it and have resurrection power. They can even give you advice on what to do and what they would do if they were you. But you have to realize that this is a storm, tailor-made and specifically designed for you. It's to take you to your next level of faith.

Reflect back to when Jesus was in the Garden of Gethsemane when He went to pray to His Father. First, he had to pull away from the disciples. Then the closer He got to the Garden of Gethsemane (the place of pressing/olive trees), He told Peter, James, and John, "Stay here and pray." They fell asleep. You have to realize that this is your storm and you can't afford to fall asleep. People are there for you as a support system. They cannot fix it for you, and they may fall asleep.

Remember the Garden of Gethsemane was full of olive trees. The oil that was used for anointing was pressed out of the olives. You have to go to the garden alone because God wants to press and crush you so He can get the precious oil out of you. In their original form, olives are beautiful. But after crushing them, they are broken into many pieces. God wants to show you through the crushing and breaking what you're made of because you don't know yourself until you're going through a storm.

Peter didn't know that he was going through a pressing when he told Jesus that he would even die with him. A few hours later, he denied Jesus three times before the rooster crowed (Matt. 26:32–35, 69–75 NKJV). Jesus knew Peter more than he knew himself. That's why Jesus told Peter, "Satan desires you. He wants to sift you like wheat. But I pray for thee that your faith would not fail thee" (Luke 22:31–32 NKJV). But in (Acts 2:31 NKJV), Peter preaches, and three thousand were saved because of the crushing process.

Continue to stand still and lean into what the scripture says about waiting. It says, "Those who wait on the Lord shall renew their strength, they shall mount up with wings like eagles, they shall run and not be weary, they shall walk and not faint" (Isa. 40:31 NKJV). And in your meantime and your waiting, "be strong and of good courage, do not fear nor be afraid of them (your storms), for the Lord your God, He is the One who goes with you. He will not leave you nor forsake you" (Deut. 31:6 NKJV)

Waiting is a lot of pressure, and I know that desperate people are moved by despair, feeling defeated or frustrated. You need to know that this is a time of pressing and crushing. It's a process and a period of time that you need to pray your way through until something supernatural happens. Like Paul, God will allow a thorn to be in your flesh just so you can know that His grace is sufficient (2 Cor. 12:7–9 NKJV). And while you're waiting, be silent, and listen to what God is saying. He is speaking to you in your darkness. Remember, you can't see any stars or the moon, and you don't know which way to go. You need to begin to command peace and calmness into your life. Remember Jesus is on the boat with you (Luke 8:22–25 NKJV). Your meantime (waiting) is to "stand still and know that He is God" (Ex. 14:13 NKJV).

Armor of God

As "standing still" relates to the Ephesians, Paul was dealing with some issues in the church at Ephesus. Some of the issues included walking in unity, spiritual gifts, not grieving the Holy Spirit, walking in love, marriage relationships, and children (Eph. 1–5 NKJV). In Ephesians 6, he tells them, "Finally my brethren." In so many words, he is saying, "If you don't remember anything else that I've told you, remember this."

His instructions were to, "be strong in the Lord and in the power of His might. Put on the whole armor of God that you may be able (Gk. Dunamis: power, ability) to stand against the wiles and schemes of the devil. For we do not wrestle against flesh and blood, but against principalities, against powers, against the rulers of the darkness of this age, against spiritual hosts of wickedness in the heavenly places. Therefore take up the whole armor of God that you may be able to withstand in the evil day" (Gk. Kakos: whatever is evil in character). "And having done all (when you've done everything else) to stand" (Eph. 6:10–13 NKJV).

When you look at the armor of God in the above verse, you can see that they represent the gear that Paul witnessed and studied while he was in the Roman prison. He studied the Roman soldiers from head to toe. On the Roman soldier's head, there was a helmet. Paul likened it to the Helmet of Salvation. His chest represented the Breastplate of Righteousness. His waist represented the Loincloth of Truth. And in one hand, he held a shield that represented the Shield of Faith. In the other hand, he held a sword that represented the Sword of the Spirit. His greaves represented having your feet shod with the Preparation of the Gospel of Peace and Prayer. The spiritual significance is in what each piece represented.

The Roman soldiers wore seven pieces of armor. The number seven represents God's perfect number. Paul was telling the Ephesians that, once you're suited up with God's armor, then you can stand against the wiles and schemes of the devil and be able to quench the fiery darts that are coming at you. Don't turn around and run. There's no armor on your back to protect you. Just stand, having sure footedness, and be like a tree planted by the rivers of the waters. Don't be moved (Ps. 1:3, Hab. 3:19 NKJV)!

Now You Can "See" (The Salvation of the Lord)

Now you can see what the Lord is going to do. You can begin to perceive with your eyes, have a mental image, visualize, understand, comprehend, believe the impossible, and apprehend that thing.

Now, let's pause for a moment. As I envision the football player on the frontline, either offensive or defensive, he is in position with his cleats implanted in the ground with his playbook plan in his mind. Now he can see clearly the direction he needs to go, staring his opponent right in the eyes. The play is called, and he waits for the signal to proceed against his opponent.

In (2 Chron. 20:17–21 NKJV), when Jehoshephat learned of a great army coming against them, he didn't seem to have a playbook until he began to talk to the one who wrote the playbook. He tells God, "We don't know what to do, but our eyes are upon You" (2 Chron. 20:12 NKJV). The spirit of the Lord came upon the prophet Jahaziel and laid out the game plan. The instructions were "do not be afraid or be dismayed of the great multitude that was going to come upon them because this battle was not theirs" (2 Chron. 20:15 NKJV). They only had to position and set themselves, stand still, and see how the Lord was going to save them and work on their behalf.

The play was called for them to go out early the next morning and believe that God would establish them and they would prosper. The play included that Jehoshephat would appoint some singers and those who would praise God. The signal was given for the singers to begin, and the Lord set ambushes against the opponent. The opponent heard the singers praising God until they got so confused that they began to turn on and destroy each other.

Because Jehoshephat and the children of Israel heard the instruction of the playbook, listened to the call, and responded to the signal, they were able to see their victory and acquired an abundance of valuables and precious jewelry from the dead bodies of the enemy. Now do you see it?

Nomi Experience

About three forty-five one afternoon, my grandson called me at work and said, "I'm lost." He had just started at a new school, and he had to catch the school bus to my brother Dion's house, which was all new to him. The bus dropped him off at an unknown destination. He kept walking in the direction in which he was used to and didn't recognize any landmarks we had instructed him to look out for. In my grandmother mode, I immediately had panic in my heart but did not let him hear the panic in my voice. I was thankful that he knew that he was lost and had enough sense to call for help.

I remained calm and asked him, "Where are you?" He responded, "I don't know." I told him to go to the nearest corner and read the street sign in both directions. After he read the signs to me, I knew exactly where he was and was able to give him further instructions. Just like your situation, God knows exactly where you are and He will come and see about you in your time of need.

I immediately took off from work and told him, "Do not move. Stand still." How many times has God told us not to move and to just stand still for I am the Lord your God? He knows the end from the beginning. I also told my grandson that I would be right there. Within minutes, I drove (flew) to where he was because I told him, "I know exactly where you are and I'll find you." Now look at this. My job was literally only seven minutes away from where the bus had dropped him off.

When I got there, the conversation went like this. "Grandma, thank you, thank you. I was lost, and you came and got me. Thank you. I'm sorry you had to leave your job." I said, "Baby, you are priority. You come first. I don't care what I'm doing. You always come first." He continued to tell me, "Thank you!"

When you're lost in your storm and you don't know which way to go, God will come and meet you where you are and save you. I don't care what He is doing at that time. He will come and see about you. You are His priority, and you come first. He will pick you up and take you where you're supposed to be. You have to stand still, let God find you, and see His salvation.

God, teach me to stand still and wait for your timing and direction. Teach me to get so grounded in You that I won't be moved by anything but Your Word. I know You have my times in Your hand and You will come and find me when I go ahead of You and get lost. You are my everything and I adore You. Your daughter. Amen!

STEP FOUR

But after long abstinence from food, then Paul stood in the midst of them and said, "Men, you should have listened to me and not have sailed from Crete and incurred this disaster and loss (Acts 27:21 NKJV).

Abstain from Food (Fasting)

The description of fasting is literally "to cover over" as the mouth (Heb. Tsum) or "to abstain from food" (Gk. Nesteia). Fasting can be observed completely for a short time or from certain foods for a longer period of time (Dan. 10:3 NKJV).

Scripture tells us that the fasting that pleases God is found in (Isa. 58:6–7 NKJV). "Is this not the fast that I have chosen; to lose the bonds of wickedness, to undo the heavy burdens, to let the oppressed go free, and that you break every yoke? Is it not to share your bread with the hungry, and that you bring to your house the poor who are cast out; when you see the naked, that you cover him, and not hide yourself from your own flesh?"

Fasting in biblical times was a spontaneous expression of grief at the time of death or great trouble. Evidence indicates that fasting also accompanied repentance. In the time of the New Testament, the Pharisees observed fasting as a ritual. The Lord told the prophet to declare to His people their transgressions or rebellion against the Lord (Is. 58:1 NKJV). The people practiced religious observances faithfully. They had fasted, but the Lord did not seem to notice. The prophet announced several reasons why the Lord had not responded to their fasting. They sought their own pleasure in fasting, they oppressed their slaves in fasting, and they quarreled and fought in their fasting.

Their fasting did not draw them closer to the Lord. The Lord wanted the kind of fast that led to doing well to others. He wanted to remind the people that they should be just and openhanded with those in need. He wanted His people to relieve the oppressed, to share their food with the hungry, and to provide housing for the poor and clothing for the naked. He wanted the Israelites to consider themselves members of one family who at one time had been slaves in Egypt. Therefore they were not to neglect each other. When someone shared with one in need, it was a reminder that everything he owned belonged to the Lord. I believe that genuine faith is focused outward in ministry and service.

(Matt. 6:16–18, Isa. 58:6-7 NKJV), tells us that fasting, in addition to prayer and good deeds are God's instructions that pleases Him, to be part of the Christian's life that are exclusively between the believer and God.

Let's look at Acts again and use your Holy Ghost imagination. (Acts 27:15 NKJV) says that, when the ship was caught and they could not head into the wind, they let her (the ship) drive or go into the direction of the waves. They next secured the skiff with great difficulty. In other words, they needed to make sure the lifeboat was stable, firm, strong, and free from any danger or loss.

I can just see them working frantically, with no rest and a determined mind, making sure they had a way of escape from the tempest-tossed ship if they had to bail. Then they had to undergird the ship with cables to make sure the bottom of the ship was stable. The next day, they had to lighten the ship. Can you hear them shouting back and forth to one another and see them throwing everything they didn't need overboard? The waves are beating on them continually without any rest. They're slipping and falling, steadily moving about with buckets to pour out the water as fast as it comes in.

On the next day, they began to throw the ship's tackle overboard with their own hands. With all this chaos going on, they didn't have time to eat or even think about it. Their focus was to be on one accord and survive this storm. They were willing to do whatever it took to accomplish this goal.

At times, you have chaos going on in your life, and you need to get a breakthrough. You need to cast out some devils and some strongholds and cast down some imaginations (2 Cor. 10:3–5 NKJV). You will need some revelation and illumination concerning your situation. Your bills need to be paid, your children need to let go of the wrong crowd, and the list goes on and on. This is no time to be thinking about eating. Warfare is going on, and you need God to begin to work on your behalf.

Look at the book of Esther, which means "star" in Persia, and you see she was displaced, orphaned, and reared by her Uncle Mordecai. Whether at his bidding, force of evil officials, or her own choice, Esther entered the beauty contest, won, and became the new queen. Mordecai's sources informed him that the Jewish people were scheduled for extinction by the wicked Haman, a self-promoter who had elevated himself to vice regent, second only to the monarch, King Ahasuerus. Faced with a desperate challenge of survival, Esther pondered Modecai's question, "Who knows whether you have come to the kingdom for such a time as this?" (Esth. 4:14 NKJV). She knew that, although the situation looked hopeless, God is never helpless.

She formulated her plan, even if it meant dying in the effort. She had prepared herself spiritually (Esth. 4:16, 9:31 NKJV). According to the tradition, she invited King Ahasuerus and Haman to a banquet. Seizing the right moment, she presented her case, not questioning the king's justice or righteousness, but humbly asking for mercy for herself and her people. With divine guidance, she had won the respect and attention of her royal husband. In response, he allowed her the responsibility of rewriting the law (Esth. 9:29 NKJV), and she became the heroine of her people. God used her beauty, intelligence, respectful attitude, as well as her faith to accomplish His will.

Here are a few examples in the Bible where they observed fasting:

- (1 Sam. 31:13, Esth. 4:1–3 NKJV), "as a sign of mourning"
- (1 Sam. 7:6, Dan. 9:3–19, Matt. 9:14–15 NKJV), as an "act of personal or corporate repentance"

- (2 Sam. 12:16–23 NKJV), as a means of "getting God's attention on behalf of suffering or sickness"
- (2 Chron. 20:1–18, EstH. 4:16, 1 Cor. 7:5 NKJV), in a "critical time of decision making"
- (2 Cor. 6:5, 11:27, Matt. 17:21 NKJV), as the "result of urgent prayer"
- (Acts 13:2–3, 14:23 NKJV), in "preparation for major events"
- (Joel 2:12–15 NKJV), "to draw closer to God"
- (Acts 10:30–33 NKJV), to "turn the believer's heart toward righteousness"
- (Luke 18:10–14, Dan. 2:23 NKJV), "not as source of spiritual pride"
- (Eph. 6:10–18 NKJV), for "spiritual warfare"

Jesus himself fasted for forty days to prepare for His ministry and to fortify His soul for confrontation with Satan (Matt. 4:1–2 NKJV). The disciples tried to heal a man's son who was an epileptic and suffered severely. He often fell into the fire and the water. They could not cure him from this demon and wondered why. Jesus responded, "However, this kind does not go out except by prayer and fasting" (Matt. 17:14–21 NKJV).

When you're going through a storm, this is the time to not only pray your way through but to abstain from food or "fast and pray" to get your breakthrough.

The fast in our text lasted for fourteen days, as did the storm. The number fourteen is the number seven twice. We know that the significance for the number seven is the number of completion. What God had in store for those who were on the ship was completed, and the power of Gold was manifested twofold.

Paul knew the power of fasting and praying and rebuked the men who did not listen to him. While fasting, you have to listen to God for clear direction. Sailing was not usually done during this time of the year, especially after September due to difficult weather. However, this particular ship set sail during the first half of October.

The same thing can happen to us. By not listening to Godly

instruction, as in (Ps. 1:1 NKJV), you can bring on your own storm. It can be the wrong time and season for what you think needs to be done in the now. And by the way, stop blaming the devil for everything. He didn't have anything to do with some of our storms. Sometimes we bring on our own disaster and loss, and then we begin to get mad when God doesn't come through for us when we want Him to. We have an attitude when people don't help us like we think they should.

Although we are talking about fasting from physical food for the nourishment and strength of our physical body so we don't starve, let's not forget about other things that can distract us from some of our breakthroughs. We can fast from the telephone, television, gossip, Facebook, twiter, credit cards, and on and on. Say ouch! Take the time to fast and pray, and watch expectantly what our God can and will do.

Father, as I go through this period of fasting, teach me Your ways and Your statutes. Show me great and mighty things, and help me to push away from life's table. Use me to Your glory, and begin to destroy things that will stop me from experiencing You. You are so awesome in my life, and I am falling more and more in love with You each day. Amen!

STEP FIVE

And now I urge you to take heart, for there will be no loss of
life among you, but only of the ship. (Acts 27:22 NKJV)

Take Heart

Take heart can be interpreted as not losing heart, do not be discouraged, having complete confidence, or not giving up. Although the travelers were in a storm, Paul heard a very encouraging word from the Lord in the night saying, "Don't be afraid." When you're going through your storm, you know beyond a shadow of a doubt, you need to hear a word. Not just any word, but one that comes alive in your spirit, a "rhema word." You need to hear a word that's going to "give you a hope and a future" (Jer. 29:11 NKJV).

Paul told the Philippians "not to be anxious or worried about anything" (Phil. 4:6 NKJV). Anything means anything. Anything means your test, your trial, your storm, your ups and downs, your ins and outs, your mountains and valleys, or whatever. He told them, but "in everything by prayer and supplication, with thanksgiving, to let your request be made known unto God." That was the prerequisite. The promise was, (Phil.4:7 NKJV) And the "peace of God" (because He's the God of peace) that surpasses all understanding will guard your hearts and minds through Christ Jesus. The key to your "peace of God" through Christ Jesus is the renewing of your heart, which is your mind.

Paul later had to encourage the Galatians in the same way God had encouraged him. He told them to "not grow weary in well doing, for in due season you shall reap if we do not lose heart" or "if we don't faint" (Gal. 6:9 NKJV). The Message/Remix Bible paraphrases it like this, "So let's not allow ourselves to get fatigued doing good. At the right time, we will harvest a good crop if we don't give up or quit." The Amplified Bible says, "And let us not lose heart and grow weary and faint in acting nobly and doing right, for in due time and at the appointed season we shall reap, if we do not loosen and relax our courage and faint."

Those on the ship were certainly weary of hard labor and wanted to give up during the storm that lasted fourteen days. They didn't have any food. Whenever the Bible tells us to do something, it is because we are lacking in that area. Paul's words to the hearers were to encourage them and build them up. Even when the ship started to sink, Paul gave words of encouragement. When Paul was being persecuted, the Lord appeared beside him and encouraged him (Acts 23:11 NKJV).

Many people are bowed down under heavy emotional loads and are weary of life's struggles. They need to hear a word of encouragement (1 Thess. 5:11 NKJV). When you're going through a storm, you need all the encouragement you can get. Not only do pleasant words taste sweet, but their use can lift us up to high places (Prov. 22:11 NKJV). Paul encourages us to take heart, be lifted up from weariness, and edify the saints, and Jesus tells us to evangelize the lost (Acts 27:22, Gal. 6:9, Eph. 4:16b, Matt. 28:19–20 NKJV).

Paul had another encouraging word to pass on to the Philippians. "Being confident of this very thing, that He who has begun a good work in you shall perform it until the day of Jesus Christ" (Phil. 1:6 NKJV). The Amplified Bible paraphrases it: "And I am convinced and sure of this very thing, that He Who began a good work in you will continue until the day of Jesus Christ (right up to the time of His return), developing (that good work) and perfecting and bringing it to full completion in you." So that means, you can't quit or lose heart any time soon. Jesus hasn't come yet.

Paul had a divine appointment, divine destiny, and divine purpose by God to get to Rome. If there had not been a storm, Paul would not have stopped to minister on the island of Malta to the natives.

While there, a poisonous snake bit Paul here, but he shook it off and continued to minister and heal many (Acts 28:1–10 NKJV).

Be Encouraged

God told Joshua, "I will be with you. I will never leave you nor forsake you. Be strong and of good courage, for to this people you shall divide as an inheritance the land which I swore to their fathers to give them. Only be strong and courageous, that you may observe to do according to all the law which Moses My servant commanded you; do not turn from it to the right hand or to the left, that you may prosper wherever you go. This book of the law shall not depart from your mouth, but you shall meditate in it day and night, that you may observe to do according to all that is written in it. For then you will make your way prosperous, and then you will have good success. Have I not commanded you? Be strong and of good courage; do not be afraid, nor be dismayed, for the Lord your God will be with you wherever you go." You have to remember that you are not alone in this. You have Jehovah Shammah with you" (Josh. 1:5-9 NKJV). This simply means, "He is there."

He told Isaiah, "When you pass through the waters, I will be with you, and through the rivers, they shall not overflow you. When you walk through the fire, you shall not be burned, nor shall the flame scorch you" (Isa. 43:2 NKJV). The Message Bible paraphrases it: "When you're in over your head, I'll be there with you. When you're in rough waters, you will not go down. When you're between a rock and a hard place, it won't be a dead end."

Take note of the word *through*. It is mentioned three times in the scripture. What is through? It means from end to end, side to side, and beginning to end. So be encouraged. The trial has a beginning, and it has an end. The first part of the Scripture says, "When you pass through."

I did a word study on the word *pass* and I got excited to see the many meanings of the word because it relates so much to these Scriptures and this chapter. I can't give you a complete description, so here are just a few. The *American Heritage Dictionary* says *pass* means to move on ahead; proceed; run. When you go through, I guarantee you will come out different than when you went in it. You will be transformed. "No test or temptation that comes your way is beyond the course of what others have to face. All you need to remember is that God will never let you down, He'll never let you be pushed past your limit, He'll always be there to help you come through it" (1 Cor. 10:13 NKJV). Remember, the trial comes just to pass, not to stay.

In Mark 6, Jairus, the ruler of the synagogue, went to Jesus and cried, "My little daughter lies at the point of death. Come and lay your hands on her, that she may be healed, and she will live." I want you to see several lessons in this verse. The point I want to make is that Jairus spoke things that were not as though they were. He spoke her healing into existence and life into his situation (Rom. 4:17b, Prov. 18:21 NKJV). He said, "Come and lay your hands on her, that she may be healed, and she will live." Remember, she was sick and at the point of death. Jesus honored Jairus's request by going with him. On their way to Jairus's house, a woman who had an issue of blood and needing a healing interrupted them.

By the time Jesus healed her and spoke with her, someone from Jairus's house came and said, "Your daughter is dead. Why trouble the Teacher any further?" Jesus remembered Jairus's request and his first words and knew he would be discouraged and lose heart. Before Jairus could speak, Jesus told him, "Do not be afraid; only believe." (Isa. 55:11 NKJV) stood really strong in this situation. It simply says, "So shall My word be that goes forth from My mouth, It shall not return to Me void. But it shall accomplish what I please, and it shall prosper in the thing for which I sent it." God's word of healing and life had been sent forth into Jairus's house, and it accomplished what it was sent to do. Jairus's little daughter was brought back to life, and his household lived happily ever after.

Another encouraging word we can glean from is when Daniel prayed to God for the sins of the people (Dan. 9 NKJV). The angel Gabriel gave him a prophecy that was so awesome and deep that he began to mourn and fast and he did not anoint himself for three full weeks. Suddenly on the twenty-fourth day, a messenger angel came and said to Daniel, "Do not fear Daniel, for from the first day that you set your heart to understand, and to humble yourself before your God, your words were heard; and I have come because of your words" (Dan. 10:12 NKJV).

On the angel's way down from heaven to give Daniel his answer of understanding, there was a great fight with the princes of Persia for twenty-one days. The messenger angel had to send for Michael the archangel to come and help him fight because he was alone. The message is, don't lose heart or be discouraged when your answer doesn't come right away. Wait for it!

When you're in a storm and you've prayed for relief, God heard you when you first prayed. Your answer, your breakthrough, and your victory are on the way. Remember, you're going through, and it has to run its course. You will stay in it until you are perfect and complete, lacking nothing (James 1:4 NKJV).

In the Fire

Ask Shadrach, Meshach, and Abednego in Daniel 3. After the three Hebrew boys did not bow down and worship the gold image at the sound of the music. They were put into the fiery furnace. King Nebuchadnezzar looked into the fiery furnace and saw four men loose, walking in the midst of the fire. They were not hurt. Their coats, trousers, turbans, and other garments were still intact. The only thing that burned up was the rope that had them bound. Remember the Scripture says they were loosed. The king also saw another person with them. He said, "The form of the fourth is like the Son of God."

You may ask, "You mean Jesus will be with me in the fire, too?"

I'm glad you asked. The answer is yes, yes, yes! Look at this. Not only will he be with you, the fire has no power over you. The three boys' hair was not even singed. Their garments were not affected, and the smell of fire was not on them. After you go through your storm, all you'll have left is a testimony. You will no longer be bound. Other than your transformation, you won't be able to tell you've been in a storm.

When you've been with the Lord, you will look, talk, and act differently. Just ask Moses when he came down from the mountaintop with a glow around his head (Ex. 34:35 NKJV). You could tell he had been with the Lord. Remember, your trial is for your perfection or completion. Your suffering will establish you and put you on a firm foundation (1 Pet. 5:10 NKJV). Your storm will make you stronger, like a tree that's planted by the rivers of waters, rooted and grounded with deep roots (Ps. 1:3 NKJV).

Here's a different perspective of being in the fire. Think of a palm tree. The taller it gets, the deeper its roots go into the ground. When a strong wind comes, the palm tree may bend or sway, but it will not fall down. When you're rooted and grounded in the word of God, a strong wind or storm can come, but it will not bring you down. "We are hard-pressed on every side, yet not crushed, we are perplexed, but not in despair, persecuted, but not forsaken, struck down, but not destroyed" (2 Cor. 4:8–9 NKJV).

This is your faith under pressure. It will be hard, but begin to consider your storm as a gift. It tests you, and challenges come at you from all sides. When you're under pressure, your faith life is forced into the open and shows its true colors. So don't try to get out of anything prematurely. It's not over until God says it is.

People will be praying for God to take you out of the storm, which is okay. But they need to agree with you on the outcome of the storm, according to the Word, and pray for your peace and wisdom while you're in the storm. Let it do its work so you become mature and well developed, not deficient or lacking in any way. God wants to stretch your faith. Trust me. When you come out of it, you will not be the same. There will always be a profit, and you need to start looking at storms differently. Storms don't come to harm you. Storms come to grow you up.

God gives you five senses and the ability to use them to see His glory. You have to keep your eyes on the Lord. Listen to Him and know His will for your life. Don't come out bitter, but come out better smelling like His sweet aroma. You have to repeat the words of David. "It was good for me that I was afflicted, that I may learn your statutes"

(Ps. 119:71 NKJV). "My tears have been my food day and night" (Ps. 42:3 NKJV).

You may feel that life has dealt you a bad hand, but play it well. Begin to feel the intangible, and start calling those things that do not exist as though they do (Rom. 4:17b NKJV). Don't limit your mind, be creative, and let God afresh you with joy. Get yourself some strategic directions, and dust off old things as they come to pass and use them as your testimony. God is pleased with your heart and faithfulness. Lift up your head, overtake, don't accept this, and lay down. I declare to you "Fight!" and "You shall pursue your breakthrough and recover all."

Let's close out this chapter with this story. A perpetrator kidnapped, raped, and beat a woman. He then bound her hands and feet with duct tape, put her in the trunk of his car, and then dumped her weary body on the side of the road. As she lay there, she began to pray to God for help. It soon started to rain while she was laying there. She continued to pray and said, "Lord, I've been kidnapped, raped, beaten, and left for dead, and now you send a storm?" As the rain continued to fall, she noticed it was getting between her skin and the duct tape. She was able to wiggle herself free. God's answer to her was, "I sent the storm to set you free" (Author unknown).

We have to remember to let our tests and trials set us free. James said to "count it all joy when you fall into various trials knowing that the testing of your faith produces patience" (James 1:2 NKJV). Your faith moves God. He wants you to become perfect and complete so you won't lack anything. In addition, if you continue to love God through your trial, you will receive the Crown of Life (James 1:12 NKJV). You won't be baldheaded when you get to heaven.

Father, here I am again, your daughter. Thank you for the word of encouragement to not lose heart as I go through my many storms and trials. I know you are there with me through everything I go through because you are El Roi, even when you are silent. You are the Great Teacher, and I trust You because You said in Your Word that You'll never leave or forsake me. I am so in love with You. Amen!

STEP SIX

*Now when the fourteenth night had come, as we were driven
up and down in the Adriatic Sea, about midnight the sailors
sensed that they were drawing near some land.*
(Acts 27:27 NKJV)

Sense That Land Is Near

We're going to look at the word *sense*. The dictionary tells us, "Intuition is the ability to sense something that is not readily evident, to know something without reducing that knowledge through reasoning."

We each have five senses: seeing, hearing, smelling, tasting, and touching. You have to touch, hear, smell, taste, and see that your storm is about to end and your breakthrough is here.

Intuition

Jesus was intuitive as He dealt with unrighteous men. He knew their thoughts, even though Jesus personally had no guile and no experience with sin (Matt. 12:25, John 6:6 NKJV). Abigail showed discerning intuition in her evaluation of the danger to her household from David and his men. In her wise intervention, she was able to protect her husband and property (1 Sam. 25:2–35 NKJV).

One of my favorite stories in the Bible is the woman with the issue of blood (Mark 6:25–34 NKJV). She heard that Jesus was in town. Although she had been plagued with her blood problem for twelve long years, she knew that, if she didn't get up from where she was, she would miss her moment for her healing. She had already spent all of her money, used up all of her resources, and couldn't get any better.

She heard enough about Jesus to know that this would be the end of her twelve-year storm. She immediately got herself up, cleaned herself as best she could, wiped her face, and got moving. She knew that, at any second, she could be stoned because of being in public with her condition, yet she was determined, and her purpose to get to Jesus was clear. She sensed and knew in her heart that her healing was near.

Keep in mind that this woman was aggressive, and she had to push some people out of her way. In pain and weakness, she tenaciously pressed her way through the crowd. She sensed that, if she missed her opportunity for her healing, her storm would not be over. She rose up with strength and kept focused, and she kept encouraging herself with every step she took.

Sailor's Intuition

In this particular passage of Scripture, because of the sailor's wise sensitivities and knowledge of the sea and its soundings, he sensed they were drawing near some land. I'm sure they were also very anxious, as well as the slaves. The Scripture says it was at midnight, the darkest part of the night, and they were still in the storm. They couldn't see anything.

Again, they had to rely on their knowledge of the sea and certain sounds that were made to let them know they were close to land and the end of their storm would be near. This is similar to when you are traveling somewhere and you begin to see certain landmarks that are familiar to you to let you know you are getting closer to your destination.

You have to know when you're coming to the end of your storm. Sense your surroundings, and know different signs and sounds, words of encouragement, and confirmations. Although each storm has its own timetable, its own season, and reason, don't forget that it comes to equip you to serve Him and it comes just to pass. Remember in step five that you don't give up or lose heart. It's almost over.

Begin to evaluate the storm with some questions. When did the storm begin? When did I start to notice the signs of the storm? What signs am I beginning to see that is letting me know (sense) the end is near?

Everybody goes through stages of the storm and different times and seasons. Some stages last longer than others. Remember that they are tailor-made for the individual. You have to do as the Scripture commands: "Stand still and see the salvation of the Lord" (2 Chron. 20 NKJV). Pay attention to the sights, sounds, and familiar landmarks. Don't move to the left or right until you see it, touch it, smell it, taste it, and know that you know this storm is over.

Now, are you ready for the final step? It might be the most difficult, yet it is the making or breaking of your victory. Sometimes, it takes a crisis (storm) to get your attention and God is going to take you to another level of your faith.

Father, thank You for showing me how to look for warning signs and landmarks in my life to know that my storm is almost over. I acknowledge that You are getting ready to take me to another level. Thank You for ordering my direction. I have waited on You and have seen many victories. Thank You God for being who You are in my life, my shepherd. Amen!

STEP SEVEN

Paul said to the centurion and the soldiers, "Unless these
men stay in the ship, you cannot be saved."
(Acts 27:31 NKJV)

Stay in the Ship

You may ask, "Why stay in the ship? There's still a storm going on in my life." Stay in the ship because Jehovah Shalom is in the ship, and his name is Jesus, the Prince of Peace. The disciples woke up Jesus when they were in a great tempest. He was asleep, and they thought He didn't care about the storm. God said, "He will give you Peace in the midst of the storm" (Matt. 8:23–27, Mark 4:35–41 NKJV). He also said, "He will give you perfect peace if your mind is stayed on Him" (Isa. 26:3 NKJV). And lastly, "The peace of God, which surpasses all understanding, will guard your hearts and minds through Christ Jesus" (Phil. 4:7 NKJV). Peace is there for you at all times.

You have to stay in the ark of safety, your ship. Gold told Noah to build an ark and his family had to stay in the ship until it was time to get out (Gen. 6–9 NKJV). Keep in mind that the total length of the flood was 365 days. Don't you think they had some anxiety? They had to send out a dove to see if the waters had receded, but they stayed in the ship (Gen. 8:8 NKJV).

When the storms of life are raging and billows are roaring, stay in the ship where there's safety. Don't jump ship. Sharks are in the water, waiting to devour you. The enemy is prowling around, seeking whom he may devour (1 Pet. 5:8 NKJV). You've got to be clearheaded and take this storm by the neck and put a chokehold on it. Don't go ahead of God or behind Him. Just stay in Him, the ship.

It is useless to try to maneuver yourself outside of God and do things on your own and wonder why you can't handle them. Sometimes we even think God is not there. Remember this. God is El Roi, and the teacher is always silent when you're taking a test. The ship represents God's perfect will, knowledge, laws, precepts, statutes, and way. "His ways are not our ways and His thoughts are not our thoughts" (Isa. 55:8 NKJV). What an awesome protective shield.

Like the disciples, it's okay to wake up your Peace and let Him "begin to do a good work in you" (Phil. 1:6 NKJV). Your storm is raging, and you can't handle it by yourself. You need some help, so stay in the ship.

"Therefore I urge you to take nourishment for this is for your survival, since not a hair will fall from the head of any of you. And when he had said these things, he took bread and gave thanks to God in the presence of them all; and when he had broken it he began to eat. Then they were all encouraged, and also took food themselves" (Acts 27:34 NKJV).

Have you seen *Are We There Yet?* starring Ice Cube? Remember everything the soon-to-be father and the two children went through to get to their destination? Their storm included many detours, a car wreck, an illegal train ride, and disappointment. They finally reached their destination, broken down from weariness and great difficulty, but they were able to rejoice at the end. Does this sound a bit like your story?

Now Eat and Give Thanks (Acts 27:34–36 NKJV)

The storm is over. Whew! Now wipe your forehead. (Ps. 30:5b NKJV) says, "Weeping may endure for a night, but joy comes in the morning." Paul and the rest of the travelers' night, was two weeks long. They didn't eat anything for fourteen days because of the storm.

When you're in a storm, you can't eat, sleep, or sometimes think straight. Sometimes we forget that God neither sleeps nor slumbers. He hasn't forgotten you. Remember, He foreknew you and predestined you. He knows the end at the beginning. So here's a bit of spiritual advice: Go to sleep and rest! Jesus told you to "cast your cares on Him because He cares for you" (1 Pet. 5:7 NKJV). Cares will keep you bent over as if you have a boulder on your back. It means you have a neurotic anxiety, which makes you nervous, and makes you have uneasy and troubled thoughts of fear about what may happen. Chill out!

A friend once told me, "When in a fix, go to Philippians 4:6 NKJV." It tells me to "be anxious for nothing (don't worry), but in everything by prayer and supplication, with thanksgiving, let your request be made known unto God." Have you ever prayed about something and then find yourself up all night worrying about it. God knew we were going to try to fix it ourselves. That's why He gave us scriptures such as these. In other words, tell God wants you to tell Him all about it and He is so complete, He will fix it. The Bible instructs us: "Let us therefore come boldly to the throne of grace (favor) that we may obtain mercy and find grace to help in the time of need" (Heb. 4:16 NKJV). Again, let God do what He does and you just stay on the ship and rest.

You have to get naked with God and remain humble. You don't have time to be timid about what you need. You have to be tenacious and begin to tell your problems how big your God is instead of telling God how big your problems are.

At dawn, the travelers began to see their joy. The sky was clear, and they could see land. I could hear them singing in my Holy Ghost imagination, "I can see clearly now. The rain is gone. I can see all obstacles in my way. Gone are the dark clouds that had me blind. It's going to be a bright, bright, sunshiny day" (Johnny Nash).

God's Purpose in the Storm

As I was watching one of our gospel stations on television, Charles Stanley was on. This one particular day, he said God's purpose in the storm was for us to let go of something, conform you to His image, and equip you to serve Him. It can destroy you or develop you. He said, "If you don't have Him, you don't have a compass. The currents of today will lead you away from God unless you hold on to the anchor."

God's Anchor

Charles Stanley said, "God's anchor comforts you in the time of the storm and is full of promise. It is God's viewpoint about what's happening to you. The anchor works when you read it. Be willing to obey it, meditate on it, believe it, and apply it to your life."

My last word to you is to dry yourself off. This storm is over. Get ready for the next one, whether it's large or small. You have the resources and equipment to go through.

Closing Prayer

Dear Father in heaven, my Lord and ruler of everything, we acknowledge you for who you are in our lives. Words can't describe. First, we want to admit our sins to you and agree with you that we have been unrighteous.

We ask that you would forgive us of all our sins of commission and omission. We ask that Your Holy Spirit would bring to our remembrance the things that we have forgotten to ask Your forgiveness for. We thank you for your promise of forgiveness, and we don't have to live in sin any longer. We thank you O God that you sent Your Son, Jesus Christ, to die on a cross that we should have died on for ourselves. We thank you that He became our sacrifice and our substitute. Now, God, we ask that you would continue to supply our needs and comfort us through our storms.

We know now through this teaching that You will be with us and, if You allowed us to go through our many storms, we would learn from them and begin to help walk alongside others to get them to the other side of their storm. We love you, adore you, magnify you, and worship you. It's in the mighty and strong name of Your Son, Jesus. Amen!

Poems

Perfect Storm

by
Aaron J. Bell, who now resides in Heaven (9/30/15)
and this poem now rests on his headstone.

It's funny how some live life going through a perfect storm,
While others struggle hard trying to do it on their own.
But as we walk through the path of eternal life
And look into the eyes of those who despise,
How can we relate if we cannot see eye to eye?
How did it get like this?
We used to be all right.
Try to show love while you're still alive,
But before you start repenting, we have to forgive to be forgiven.
Remember, it was written,
So let's start living with no worries, no sorrows.
Give thanks day to day.
Don't save love for tomorrow.
'Cause when it's all said and done and there's no one to turn to,
God's love will always protect you,
For many have gone through the storm, too.

The Eye of the Storm

by
Karen Walker

Trouble, it comes test, trials, of the enemies attack,
Distressing my life, throwing me off track,
Hindering me from my God-given call that I
must do something to prevent the fall.
So I get busy trying to fix my life,
Putting my hands in God's business, like
I know how to win this fight,
Only to have my life torn into shreds.
Brokenhearted and ashamed, I hang my head.
Then I heard a voice say, "Find the eye of
the storm. Stand still and know
that I am God. I will never leave you nor forsake you!"
But did I listen?
Of course not!
Running here and there like a chicken with my head cut off,
Trying to find all the pieces that the storm had tossed,
Gathering them all together in one big, huge pile,
Not seeing the enemy's imps eyeing me all the while,
Waiting to prance on my life once again.
I see them now, and this fight they won't win.
Then I remember the words the Lord spoke to me,
"Find the eye of the storm, and there you'll find me."
So down on my knees with my head bowed down,
I stayed right there 'til my Lord I had found.
I listened once again as He spoke to me,
"Find the eye of the storm, and there you'll find me."
To the eye of the storm, my feet ran so fast.
When I look back, now I ran through my past.

I planted myself right where the Lord told me,
And when I opened my eyes,
The I became we.
For the eye of the storm,
My Father was waiting for my life to transform.

Testimonials

My storm is over. I was just like the woman who had been bent over for eighteen years and could not lift herself up. I was in a dark place and didn't know which way to move, so I stood still in a paralytic state. It took some friends to take me out for some ice cream and talk to me so I could see my situation from a different perspective.

As I began to see myself, from the outside looking in, I didn't like what I saw. I was pitiful, locked into a situation that was sucking the life out of me. I knew that God did not want this for His daughter. I had to drop some things and I also learned that, when we complain, we remain, but, when we praise, we will be raised. I followed the seven steps of this book, and I am at a different place in my life, living peaceful and victorious. I know other storms will come, but now I know how to go through them. On September 30, 2015, my son Aaron J. Bell passed away. Although I knew other storms would inevitably be coming, I did not know this storm was in my forecast. Although I am in pain, I also have peace, knowing that Aaron is in the loving arms of the Lord.

Marcia

God brought me through a major storm. When my son passed in 2012, I did not know what was to come next. I kept my eyes on God, surrounded myself with positive people and those who weren't meant to stick around, fell off the wagon. It has not always been a smooth ride, but today 4 years later, I am stronger, wiser and much closer to

God. Even when I thought He left me, He was right there. His purpose for me has been greatly revealed through this process and I have a better understanding of life in general. Healing is still taking place, but it looks different now. Hard to explain, but I am glad He chose me for this storm.

Brianna Monique

My storm was full of drugs that took control of my life. It stole time from my family, especially my child and the church. I believed that my family had turned their backs on me and didn't want to be around me. I knew God was calling me, although I knew I was breaking God's heart. One Saturday night at church, I threw myself on the altar, and I was ready to walk away, lay it down, and give it all up. I heard God's voice saying, "Your walk is all wrong."

I began to grow tired of going through the same old stuff again and again and realized I had to trust God and allow Him to be God. I am so thankful to God, who knows my heart and knew a battle was happening on the inside.

I finally stopped using, and I admit I still had urges to look back. But here I am today, seven years later, delivered for real. I'm washed in the blood of the Lamb. Praise God.

Karen Lynette

Afterword

Sometimes, you will find yourself going through life's storms and winds. You will be tossed to and fro, and it will seem as though it's hard to handle or manage. Make sure that you act on the words of the old hymn. "Make sure your anchor holds, and grip a solid rock." The climax of the song says, "This rock is Jesus." (Ps. 1:3 NKJV) says, "You will be like a tree planted by the rivers of water." I want you to picture a palm tree. The higher the palm tree grows, the deeper the roots go so it will not be uprooted. The winds can come and blow as hard as they want to, and the tree itself may bend and sway, but it will not break. I promise you, you won't break.

Paul's story tells us that the season for sailing was over, much time had been lost, and navigation was already dangerous. Paul had some insight on the upcoming events that were about to happen. He knew the voyage was not going to be safe. Likewise, God may give us a peek into future events (warning signs or weather conditions) that we should not ignore.

Remember what happened in the movie *The Perfect Storm*, how the owner and helmsman (pilot) were determined to go out to sea, even in stormy weather, against the wind and waves. Although the crew was frightened, they tried to be strong. The entire crew ended up dying in the storm and did exactly what Paul was trying to prevent.

So what does all this mean? Keep this thought in mind. If you, a friend, or a loved one is going through a storm, don't worry about getting a little wet. Just dance in the rain and remember the storm comes to pass. It doesn't come to stay.

Conclusion

Jesus continues to sit at the right hand of the Father, interceding for you (Heb. 7:25 NKJV), praying for you (Mark 6:46 NKJV), and seeing you struggling (Mark 6:48 NKJV). He sees you when you're scared and feel that you're all alone (Matt. 14:23, 26 NKJV). He will reveal Himself (Mark 6:50 NKJV) and give you courage and confidence (Mark 6:50–51, Matt. 14:33 NKJV). You will be able to help bring others through after you have successfully come through your storm. Jesus told the disciples, "Bring all who were sick ... that they might only touch the hem of His garment (Matt. 14:35–36 NKJV).

The potential you have for maturing relates to you recognizing that you have a God-given destiny. You are striving to reach a goal and a purpose that only God can enable you to achieve. We can learn many lessons from a storm. We have to realize that God is in control, and this is what's needed in your life to mature you and make you humble and godly. (Rom. 8:28 NKJV) states, "And we know that all things work together for good to those who love God, to those who are the called according to His purpose. For whom He foreknew, He also predestined to be conformed to the image of His Son, that He might be the firstborn among many brethren. Moreover whom He predestined, these He also called; whom He called, He also justified; and whom He justified, He also glorified."

"The end of a thing is better than its beginning" (Eccl. 7:8 NKJV). We need to understand that nothing takes God by surprise. He knew way back through eternity what you were going to go through. It's difficult going through right now, but remember, "God will give you

Peace (Jesus) in the midst of the storm" (Mark 4:39 NKJV). And again, He knows the end from the beginning. God Himself is our Peace (Eph. 2:14 NKJV). Keep these thoughts in your heart as you go through your storm.

Bibliography

Life's experiences

New King James Version. *The Nelson Study Bible*. Thomas Nelson, 1882.

Strong, James. *Strong's Exhaustive Concordance of the Bible*. Hendrickson.

The New King James Version. *The Woman's Study Bible*. Thomas Nelson, 1995.

The New Ungers Bible Dictionary. Moody Press.

The World Book Dictionary.

Towns, Elmer L. *A Journey through the New Testament: A Worktext. The Story of Christ and How He Developed the Church*.

Vine, W.E. *Vine's Expository Dictionary of Old and New Testament Words*. Nelson's Super Value Series.

Zondervan Amplified Bible. *The Original Greek and Hebrew*.

About the Author

Marcia Christian Bell is a mother of five, grandmother of nine, and has completed her biblical education through Valor Christian College, A. A. S. in Pastoral Leadership (Rod Parsley). She also attended Liberty University's School of Religion and Fresno Pacific University in biblical and religious studies.

She has also attended and completed a two-year course at the Sound Doctrine Bible School at the West Fresno Baptist Church. Some of her past experiences include but not limited to serving as Vacation Bible School co-director, Essentials of New Life classes, Sunday school teacher, prayer warrior and elder.

She has also served as a speaker for seminars and workshops for the last twenty-five years and birthed many ministries that have helped the lives of many. She's also a writer and producer of various dramatizations in the worship and arts field.

Her passion is helping others discover their spiritual gifts and find where they can assimilate into ministry. But most of all, she is in love with the lover of her soul, Jesus Christ.

Printed in the United States
By Bookmasters